All rights reserved. This book or any portion thereof
may not be reproduced or used in any manner whatsoever without the express written permission of the
publisher.
River Breeze Press 2018 First Printing

This journal belongs to:

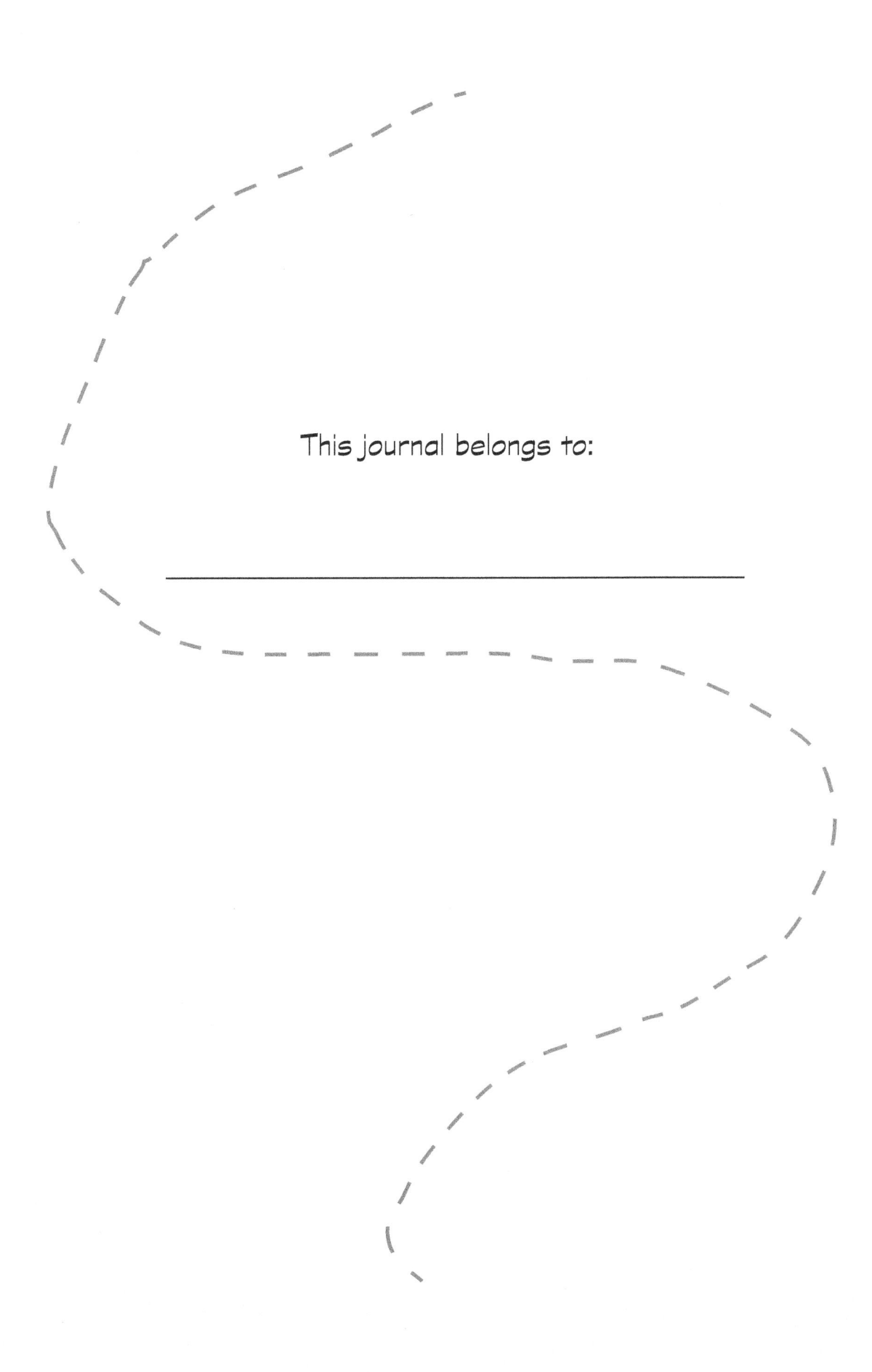

_____

Today we went to: _____

Date: _____   Location: _____

Today is: Monday Tuesday Wednesday Thursday Friday Saturday Sunday

Weather
Temperature: _____

_____
_____
_____

Draw the best thing about today:

List something that you

heard: _____

smelled: _____

ate: _____

What did you see or do? _____

_____
_____
_____
_____
_____
_____
_____
_____

Today's Overall Rating
☆ ☆ ☆ ☆ ☆

Today we went to: _____

Date: _____   Location: _____

Today is: Monday Tuesday Wednesday Thursday Friday Saturday Sunday

Weather

Temperature: _____

_____
_____
_____

Draw the best thing about today:

List something that you

heard: _____

smelled: _____

ate: _____

What did you see or do? _____

_____
_____
_____
_____
_____
_____
_____
_____

Today's Overall Rating
☆ ☆ ☆ ☆ ☆

Today we went to: _____

Date: _____   Location: _____

Today is: Monday Tuesday Wednesday Thursday Friday Saturday Sunday

Weather

Temperature: _____

_____
_____
_____

Draw the best thing about today:

List something that you

heard: _____

smelled: _____

ate: _____

What did you see or do? _____

_____
_____
_____
_____
_____
_____
_____
_____

Today's Overall Rating
☆ ☆ ☆ ☆ ☆

Today we went to: _____

Date: _____   Location: _____

Today is: Monday Tuesday Wednesday Thursday Friday Saturday Sunday

Weather

Temperature: _____

_____
_____
_____

Draw the best thing about today:

List something that you

heard: _____

smelled: _____

ate: _____

What did you see or do? _____

_____
_____
_____
_____
_____
_____
_____

Today's Overall Rating
☆ ☆ ☆ ☆ ☆

Today we went to: _____

Date: _____   Location: _____

Today is: Monday Tuesday Wednesday Thursday Friday Saturday Sunday

Weather

Temperature: _____

_____
_____
_____

Draw the best thing about today:

List something that you

heard: _____

smelled: _____

ate: _____

What did you see or do? _____

_____
_____
_____
_____
_____
_____
_____
_____

Today's Overall Rating
☆ ☆ ☆ ☆ ☆

Today we went to: _____

Date: _____   Location: _____

Today is: Monday Tuesday Wednesday Thursday Friday Saturday Sunday

Weather

Temperature: _____

_____
_____
_____

Draw the best thing about today:

List something that you

heard: _____

smelled: _____

ate: _____

What did you see or do? _____

_____
_____
_____
_____
_____
_____
_____

Today's Overall Rating
☆ ☆ ☆ ☆ ☆

Today we went to: _____

Date: _____ Location: _____

Today is: Monday Tuesday Wednesday Thursday Friday Saturday Sunday

Weather

Temperature: _____

_____
_____
_____

Draw the best thing about today:

List something that you

heard: _____

smelled: _____

ate: _____

What did you see or do? _____

_____
_____
_____
_____
_____
_____
_____

Today's Overall Rating
☆ ☆ ☆ ☆ ☆

Today we went to: _____

Date: _____   Location: _____

Today is: Monday Tuesday Wednesday Thursday Friday Saturday Sunday

Weather

Temperature: _____

_____
_____
_____

Draw the best thing about today:

List something that you

heard: _____

smelled: _____

ate: _____

What did you see or do? _____

_____
_____
_____
_____
_____
_____
_____
_____

Today's Overall Rating
☆ ☆ ☆ ☆ ☆

Today we went to: _____

Date: _____   Location: _____

Today is: Monday Tuesday Wednesday Thursday Friday Saturday Sunday

Weather

Temperature: _____

_____
_____
_____

Draw the best thing about today:

List something that you

heard: _____

smelled: _____

ate: _____

What did you see or do? _____

_____
_____
_____
_____
_____
_____
_____
_____

Today's Overall Rating
☆ ☆ ☆ ☆ ☆

Today we went to: _____

Date: _____   Location: _____

Today is: Monday Tuesday Wednesday Thursday Friday Saturday Sunday

Weather

Temperature: _____

_____
_____
_____

Draw the best thing about today:

List something that you

heard: _____

smelled: _____

ate: _____

What did you see or do? _____

_____
_____
_____
_____
_____
_____
_____
_____

Today's Overall Rating
☆ ☆ ☆ ☆ ☆

Today we went to: _____

Date: _____   Location: _____

Today is: Monday Tuesday Wednesday Thursday Friday Saturday Sunday

Weather
Temperature: _____

_____
_____
_____

Draw the best thing about today:

List something that you

heard: _____

smelled: _____

ate: _____

What did you see or do? _____
_____
_____
_____
_____
_____
_____
_____

Today's Overall Rating
☆ ☆ ☆ ☆ ☆

Today we went to: _____

Date: _____   Location: _____

Today is: Monday Tuesday Wednesday Thursday Friday Saturday Sunday

Weather
Temperature: _____

_____
_____
_____

Draw the best thing about today:

List something that you

heard: _____

smelled: _____

ate: _____

What did you see or do? _____

_____
_____
_____
_____
_____
_____
_____

Today's Overall Rating
☆ ☆ ☆ ☆ ☆

Today we went to: _____

Date: _____   Location: _____

Today is: Monday Tuesday Wednesday Thursday Friday Saturday Sunday

Weather

Temperature: _____

_____
_____
_____

Draw the best thing about today:

List something that you

heard: _____

smelled: _____

ate: _____

What did you see or do? _____

_____
_____
_____
_____
_____
_____
_____
_____

Today's Overall Rating
☆ ☆ ☆ ☆ ☆

Today we went to: _____

Date: _____   Location: _____

Today is: Monday Tuesday Wednesday Thursday Friday Saturday Sunday

Weather
Temperature: _____

_____
_____
_____

Draw the best thing about today:

List something that you

heard: _____

smelled: _____

ate: _____

What did you see or do? _____

_____
_____
_____
_____
_____
_____
_____
_____

Today's Overall Rating
☆ ☆ ☆ ☆ ☆

Today we went to: _____

Date: _____   Location: _____

Today is: Monday Tuesday Wednesday Thursday Friday Saturday Sunday

Weather

Temperature: _____

_____
_____
_____

Draw the best thing about today:

List something that you

heard: _____

smelled: _____

ate: _____

What did you see or do? _____

_____
_____
_____
_____
_____
_____
_____
_____

Today's Overall Rating
☆ ☆ ☆ ☆ ☆

Today we went to: _____

Date: _____ Location: _____

Today is: Monday Tuesday Wednesday Thursday Friday Saturday Sunday

Weather
Temperature: _____

_____
_____
_____

Draw the best thing about today:

List something that you

heard: _____

smelled: _____

ate: _____

What did you see or do? _____

_____
_____
_____
_____
_____
_____
_____

Today's Overall Rating
☆ ☆ ☆ ☆ ☆

Today we went to: _____

Date: _____   Location: _____

Today is: Monday Tuesday Wednesday Thursday Friday Saturday Sunday

Weather

Temperature: _____

☀️ ⛅🌦 ☁️ 🌧

_____
_____
_____

Draw the best thing about today:

List something that you

heard: _____

smelled: _____

ate: _____

What did you see or do? _____

_____
_____
_____
_____
_____
_____
_____
_____

Today's Overall Rating
☆ ☆ ☆ ☆ ☆

Today we went to: _____

Date: _____   Location: _____

Today is: Monday Tuesday Wednesday Thursday Friday Saturday Sunday

Weather

Temperature: _____

_____
_____
_____

Draw the best thing about today:

List something that you

heard: _____

smelled: _____

ate: _____

What did you see or do? _____

_____
_____
_____
_____
_____
_____
_____

Today's Overall Rating
☆ ☆ ☆ ☆ ☆

Today we went to: _____

Date: _____   Location: _____

Today is: Monday Tuesday Wednesday Thursday Friday Saturday Sunday

Weather

Temperature: _____

_____
_____
_____

Draw the best thing about today:

List something that you

heard: _____

smelled: _____

ate: _____

What did you see or do? _____

_____
_____
_____
_____
_____
_____
_____

Today's Overall Rating
☆ ☆ ☆ ☆ ☆

Today we went to: _____

Date: _____   Location: _____

Today is: Monday Tuesday Wednesday Thursday Friday Saturday Sunday

Weather
Temperature: _____

_____
_____
_____

Draw the best thing about today:

List something that you

heard: _____

smelled: _____

ate: _____

What did you see or do? _____

_____
_____
_____
_____
_____
_____

Today's Overall Rating
☆ ☆ ☆ ☆ ☆

Today we went to: _____

Date: _____ Location: _____

Today is: Monday Tuesday Wednesday Thursday Friday Saturday Sunday

Weather

Temperature: _____

_____
_____
_____

Draw the best thing about today:

List something that you

heard: _____

smelled: _____

ate: _____

What did you see or do? _____

_____
_____
_____
_____
_____
_____
_____
_____

Today's Overall Rating
☆ ☆ ☆ ☆ ☆

Today we went to: _____

Date: _____   Location: _____

Today is: Monday Tuesday Wednesday Thursday Friday Saturday Sunday

Weather
Temperature: _____

_____
_____
_____

Draw the best thing about today:

List something that you

heard: _____

smelled: _____

ate: _____

What did you see or do? _____

_____
_____
_____
_____
_____
_____
_____

Today's Overall Rating
☆ ☆ ☆ ☆ ☆

Today we went to: _____

Date: _____   Location: _____

Today is: Monday Tuesday Wednesday Thursday Friday Saturday Sunday

Weather

Temperature: _____

_____
_____
_____

Draw the best thing about today:

List something that you

heard: _____

smelled: _____

ate: _____

What did you see or do? _____

_____
_____
_____
_____
_____
_____
_____
_____

Today's Overall Rating
☆ ☆ ☆ ☆ ☆

Today we went to: _____

Date: _____   Location: _____

Today is: Monday Tuesday Wednesday Thursday Friday Saturday Sunday

Weather

Temperature: _____

_____
_____
_____

Draw the best thing about today:

List something that you

heard: _____

smelled: _____

ate: _____

What did you see or do? _____

_____
_____
_____
_____
_____
_____
_____

Today's Overall Rating
☆ ☆ ☆ ☆ ☆

Today we went to: _____

Date: _____   Location: _____

Today is: Monday Tuesday Wednesday Thursday Friday Saturday Sunday

Weather

Temperature: _____

☀️ 🌦️ ☁️ 🌧️

_____
_____
_____

Draw the best thing about today:

List something that you

heard: _____

smelled: _____

ate: _____

What did you see or do? _____

_____
_____
_____
_____
_____
_____
_____

Today's Overall Rating
☆ ☆ ☆ ☆ ☆

Today we went to: _____

Date: _____ Location: _____

Today is: Monday Tuesday Wednesday Thursday Friday Saturday Sunday

Weather
Temperature: _____

_____
_____
_____

Draw the best thing about today:

List something that you

heard: _____

smelled: _____

ate: _____

What did you see or do? _____

_____
_____
_____
_____
_____
_____
_____
_____

Today's Overall Rating
☆ ☆ ☆ ☆ ☆

Today we went to: _____

Date: _____   Location: _____

Today is: Monday Tuesday Wednesday Thursday Friday Saturday Sunday

Weather
Temperature: _____

_____
_____
_____

Draw the best thing about today:

List something that you

heard: _____

smelled: _____

ate: _____

What did you see or do? _____

_____
_____
_____
_____
_____
_____
_____
_____

Today's Overall Rating
☆ ☆ ☆ ☆ ☆

Today we went to: _____

Date: _____   Location: _____

Today is: Monday Tuesday Wednesday Thursday Friday Saturday Sunday

Weather

Temperature: _____

_____
_____
_____

Draw the best thing about today:

List something that you

heard: _____

smelled: _____

ate: _____

What did you see or do? _____

_____
_____
_____
_____
_____
_____
_____
_____

Today's Overall Rating

☆ ☆ ☆ ☆ ☆

Today we went to: _____

Date: _____   Location: _____

Today is: Monday Tuesday Wednesday Thursday Friday Saturday Sunday

Weather

Temperature: _____

☀ ⛅ ☁ 🌧

_____
_____
_____

Draw the best thing about today:

List something that you

heard: _____

smelled: _____

ate: _____

What did you see or do? _____

_____
_____
_____
_____
_____
_____
_____

Today's Overall Rating
☆ ☆ ☆ ☆ ☆

Today we went to: _____

Date: _____ Location: _____

Today is: Monday Tuesday Wednesday Thursday Friday Saturday Sunday

Weather

Temperature: _____

☀️ ⛅ ☁️ 🌧️

_____
_____
_____

Draw the best thing about today:

List something that you

heard: _____

smelled: _____

ate: _____

What did you see or do? _____

_____
_____
_____
_____
_____
_____
_____

Today's Overall Rating
☆ ☆ ☆ ☆ ☆

Today we went to: _____

Date: _____ Location: _____

Today is: Monday Tuesday Wednesday Thursday Friday Saturday Sunday

Weather

Temperature: _____

_____
_____
_____

Draw the best thing about today:

List something that you

heard: _____

smelled: _____

ate: _____

What did you see or do? _____

_____
_____
_____
_____
_____
_____
_____

Today's Overall Rating
☆ ☆ ☆ ☆ ☆

Today we went to: _____

Date: _____   Location: _____

Today is: Monday Tuesday Wednesday Thursday Friday Saturday Sunday

Weather
Temperature: _____

_____
_____
_____

Draw the best thing about today:

List something that you

heard: _____

smelled: _____

ate: _____

What did you see or do? _____

_____
_____
_____
_____
_____
_____
_____
_____

Today's Overall Rating
☆ ☆ ☆ ☆ ☆

Today we went to: _____

Date: _____ Location: _____

Today is: Monday Tuesday Wednesday Thursday Friday Saturday Sunday

Weather

Temperature: _____

_____
_____
_____

Draw the best thing about today:

List something that you

heard: _____

smelled: _____

ate: _____

What did you see or do? _____

_____
_____
_____
_____
_____
_____
_____

Today's Overall Rating
☆ ☆ ☆ ☆ ☆

Today we went to: _____

Date: _____   Location: _____

Today is: Monday Tuesday Wednesday Thursday Friday Saturday Sunday

Weather

Temperature: _____

_____
_____
_____

Draw the best thing about today:

List something that you

heard: _____

smelled: _____

ate: _____

What did you see or do? _____

_____
_____
_____
_____
_____
_____
_____
_____

Today's Overall Rating
☆ ☆ ☆ ☆ ☆

Made in the USA
Middletown, DE
17 February 2019